D0408255

VICTORIA'S SECRET

GARDENS OF LOVE

GARDENS

⤸ OF ⤷

LOVE

VOLUME THREE

Authorized *Purveyors*

VICTORIA'S SECRET

Nº 10 MARGARET STREET
LONDON W1

FOR AS LONG as lovers and poets have sung of their loves, of their passions, hopes and yearnings, they have found that the world of nature is the perfect mirror for the world of their emotions. Nothing but nature's transient moods and changing seasons can reflect the mutability and variety of love's emotions; and nothing but the beauties of flowers can equal or express the loved one's charms. It is no coincidence that the earliest love story in western literature took place in a garden: Paradise imagined in seductive detail by John Milton: 'Here in close recess, with flowers, garlands, and sweet‑smelling herbs, espoused Eve deck'd first her nuptial bed.'

Milton's great hymn to love is only one of the pieces of verse and prose I have chosen for this treasury, reflecting all the moods and seasons of the Garden of Love. The springtime of love, in all its sweet simplicity, is here expressed in the delighted impatience of the Elizabethan sonnets, the tender lyricism of the eighteenth‑century Romantics and the artless innocence of Victorian valentines.

Love's blossoming – sometimes delicate and hesitant, sometimes overwhelming in its passion – can be found in the summertime idylls of Rossetti and Ann Radcliffe, and in the still, sultry evenings described by Charlotte Brontë and

Thomas Hardy. The urgent, unspoken emotion in Jane Eyre's encounter with Mr Rochester, and the poignancy of Eustacia Vyne's parting from Clym, are evoked almost entirely by the details of the landscapes that surround them.

Here too I have included the autumn of love: the ripeness and fruition of love reflected in the bounty of golden apples described by Elizabeth Gaskell, and the serenity and mellow comfort of mature love, captured by Vita Sackville-West. And there are of course the torments, the delicious doubts and mysteries of love, reflected in nature's April showers and summer storms – and in the inexorable waning of the autumn sun and the approach of winter's frosts.

This beautiful and moving imagery from the world of nature has proved as irresistible to painters down the centuries as it has to poets and novelists. Thus each of these lovely pieces of verse and prose has found its pair in an image which I feel perfectly reflects its mood and its charm. Together they capture not only the delights and ecstasies of love, but also that delirious feeling – known by all true lovers – of being in touch with the infinite, and in sympathy with all creation; for in lovers' eyes, as in Shelley's, the irresistible power of love governs the world and its creatures:

> Nothing in the world is single;
>   All things by a law divine
> In one another's being mingle: –
>   Why not I with thine?

With Love

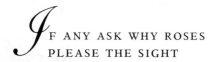

*I*F ANY ASK WHY ROSES PLEASE THE SIGHT

If any ask why roses please the sight?
Because their leaves upon thy cheeks do bower:
If any ask why lilies are so white?
Because their blossoms in thy hand do flower:
Or why sweet plants so grateful odours shower?
   It is because thy breath so like they be:
   Or why the orient sun so bright we see?
What reason can we give, but from thine eyes, and thee?

GILES FLETCHER 1588?–1623

OVE

Love found you still a child,
Who looked on him and smiled
Scornful with laughter mild
   And knew him not:
Love turned and looked on you,
Love looked and he smiled too,
And all at once you knew
   You knew not what.

Love laughed again, and said
Smiling, 'Be not afraid:
Though lord of all things made,
   I do no wrong:
Like you I love all flowers,
All dusky twilight hours,
Spring sunshine and spring showers,
   Like you am young.'

Love took you by the hand
At eve, and bade you stand
At edge of the woodland,
   Where I should pass;
Love sent me thither, sweet,
And brought me to your feet;
He willed that we should meet,
   And so it was.

JOHN BOWYER BUCHANAN NICHOLS 1859–1939

Ophelia's Song

How should I your true love know from another one?
By his cockle hat and staff, and his sandal shoon.

He is dead and gone, lady, he is dead and gone,
At his head a grass-green turf, at his heels a stone.

> White his shroud as the mountain snow,
> Larded with sweet flowers:
> Which bewept to the grave did go,
> With true-love showers.

WILLIAM SHAKESPEARE 1564–1616

I MUST NOT TELL,
HOW DEAR
YOU ARE TO ME

I must not tell, how dear you are to me.
It is unknown, as secret from myself
Who should know best. I would not if I could
Expose the meaning of such mystery.

I loved you then, when love was spring, and May.
Eternity is here and now, I thought;
The June and perfect moment briefly caught
As in your arms, but still a child, I lay.

Loved you when summer deepened into June
And those fair, wild, ideal dreams of youth
Were true yet dangerous and half unreal
As when Endymion kissed the mateless moon.

But now when autumn yellows all the leaves
And thirty seasons mellow on long love,
How rooted, how secure, how strong, how rich,
How full the barn that holds our summered sheaves!

V. SACKVILLE-WEST 1892–1962

WAITING FOR DAISY

The girls gradually came out on to the lawn. I began to fear that Daisy was not coming. She was the last of all. I was horribly afraid she had been advised not to appear, because I was there. Presently I turned and there she was in a black velvet jacket and light dress, with a white feather in her hat and her bright golden hair tied up with blue riband. How bright and fresh and happy and pretty she looked . . .

. . . I love her more and more each time I see her. I think she loves me a little. I hope so. God grant it. I am sure she does not dislike me, and I believe, I do believe, she likes me and cares for me. I fancy I can see it in her clear loving deep grey eyes, so true and fearless and honest, those beautiful Welsh eyes that seem to like to meet mine. I think she likes to be with me and talk with me, or why did she come back to me again and again and stand by me and talk to no one else? I wish I could tell her how dearly I love her but I dare not.

REV. FRANCIS KILVERT 1840–79

*S*PRING

Say over again, and yet once over again
   That thou dost love me. Though the word repeated
   Should seem 'a cuckoo song', as thou dost treat it,
Remember, never to the hill or plain,
Valley and wood, without her cuckoo-strain,
   Comes the fresh Spring in all her green completed.
   Beloved, I, amid the darkness greeted
By a doubtful spirit-voice, in that doubt's pain
   Cry, 'Speak once more . . . thou lovest!' Who can fear
Too many stars, though each in heaven shall roll,
   Too many flowers, though each shall crown the year?
Say thou dost love me, love me, love me – toll
   The silver iterance! – only minding, Dear,
To love me also in silence, with thy soul.

ELIZABETH BARRETT BROWNING 1806–61

$\mathcal{G}$ATHERING PEACHES

Behold, wherever she does pass,
  How all the amorous trees contend
Whose loaded arms should her embrace,
  While with their fruit tow'rds her they bend,
    As if the willing branches meant
    To her their bounty to present.

The upper boughs, all bending low,
   Her raisëd arm seem to prevent;
While those that level with her grow
    To meet her easy hand consent:
      To court her thus, Lo! every peach
      Submits itself, within her reach.

These she prefers, refusing those,
   Unhappy, in their ripening last;
Persuaded by her eye to choose,
    As that the coloured fruit does taste;
      Which her desire does gently move
      To what her sense did first approve.

Fair as this golden fruit here seems,
   The sun, with kind salutes, thus streaks,
And, gilding them with amorous beams,
    Prints purple kisses on their cheeks –
      Kisses soft as that tender down
      Which their young blushing cheeks does crown.

Ah, could the Fair, who this does see,
   Be by this great example won,
And learn but thus to smile on me
    As *they* smile on the kissing sun!
      Bright as their cheeks with kisses shine,
      Hers brighter should appear with mine.

RICHARD LEIGH 1649–

FIRST LOVE

I ne'er was struck before that hour
   With love so sudden and so sweet,
Her face it bloomed like a sweet flower
And stole my heart away complete.
My face turned pale as deadly pale,
   My legs refused to walk away,
And when she looked, what could I ail?
   My life and all seemed turned to clay.

And then my blood rushed to my face
   And took my eyesight quite away,
The trees and bushes round the place
   Seemed midnight at noonday.
I could not see a single thing,
   Words from my eyes did start —
They spoke as chords do from the string,
   And blood burnt round my heart.

Are flowers the winter's choice?
   Is love's bed always snow?
She seemed to hear my silent voice,
   Not love's appeals to know.
I never saw so sweet a face
   As that I stood before.
My heart has left its dwelling-place
   And can return no more.

JOHN CLARE 1793—1864

TURN I MY LOOKS

Turn I my looks unto the skies,
Love with his arrows wounds mine eyes;
If so I gaze upon the ground,
Love then in every flower is found;
Search I the shade to fly the pain,
He meets me in the shade again;
Wend I to walk in sacred grove,
Even there I meet with sacred Love;
If so I bain me in the spring,
Even on the bank I hear him sing;
If so I meditate alone,
He will be partner of my moan;
If so I mourn, he weeps with me,
And where I am there he will be.

THOMAS LODGE ?1558—1625

LOUISA

I met Louisa in the shade,
And, having seen that lovely Maid,
Why should I fear to say
That, nymph-like, she is fleet and strong,
And down the rocks can leap along
Like rivulets in May?

And she hath smiles to earth unknown;
Smiles, that with motion of their own
Do spread, and sink, and rise;
That come and go with endless play,
And ever, as they pass away,
Are hidden in her eyes.

She loves her fire, her cottage-home;
Yet o'er the moorland will she roam
In weather rough and bleak;
And, when against the wind she strains,
Oh! might I kiss the mountain rains
That sparkle on her cheek.

Take all that's mine 'beneath the moon,'
If I with her but half a noon
May sit beneath the walls
Of some old cave, or mossy nook,
When up she winds along the brook
To hunt the waterfalls.

WILLIAM WORDSWORTH 1770—1850

 WHITE ROSE

The red rose whispers of passion,
   And the white rose breathes of love;
O, the red rose is a falcon,
   And the white rose is a dove.

But I send you a cream-white rosebud
   With a flush on its petal tips;
For the love that is purest and sweetest
   Has a kiss of desire on the lips.

JOHN BOYLE O'REILLY 1844–90

*F*LOWERS BENEATH HER FEET

This is the birthday of my Love,
    Then vanish care and sorrow;
To-day shall mirth and pleasure reign,
    Tho' grief should come tomorrow.
My Love draws near with airy tread,
    And glances shy and sweet;
Sing, little birds, above her head,
    Bloom, flowers, beneath her feet.

ANONYMOUS NINETEENTH CENTURY

GENTLE STREAMS

Glide, gentle streams, and bear
Along with you my tear
  To that coy girl
  Who smiles, yet slays
  Me with delays;
And strings my tears as pearl.

ROBERT HERRICK 1591–1674

THE GARDEN

Fair Quiet, have I found thee here,
And Innocence, thy sister dear!
Mistaken long, I sought you then
In busy companies of men.
Your sacred plants, if here below,
Only among the plants will grow.
Society is all but rude,
To this delicious solitude.

No white nor red was ever seen
So am'rous as this lovely green.
Fond lovers, cruel as their flame,
Cut in these trees their mistress' name.
Little, alas, they know, or heed,
How far these beauties hers exceed!
Fair trees! wheres'e'er your barks I wound,
No name shall but your own be found.

· ◇ ·

When we have run our passion's heat,
Love hither makes his best retreat.
The gods, that mortal beauty chase,
Still in a tree did end their race.
Apollo hunted Daphne so,
Only that she might laurel grow.
And Pan did after Syrinx speed,
Not as a nymph, but for a reed.

· ◇ ·

What wondrous life is this I lead!
Ripe apples drop about my head;
The luscious clusters of the vine
Upon my mouth do crush their wine;
The nectarene, and curious peach,
Into my hands themselves do reach;
Stumbling on melons, as I pass,
Ensnared with flowers, I fall on grass.

· ◇ ·

Meanwhile the mind, from pleasures less,
Withdraws into its happiness:
The mind, that ocean where each kind
Does straight its own resemblance find,
Yet it creates, transcending these,
Far other worlds, and other seas,
Annihilating all that's made
To a green thought in a green shade.

ANDREW MARVELL 1621–78

IN THE ORCHARD

It was one mid-day that both of us being on the line near Heathbridge, and knowing that they were gathering apples at the farm, we resolved to spend the men's dinner-hour in going over there. We found the great clothes-baskets full of apples and stopping up the way; and an universal air of merry contentment with this the final produce of the year. The yellow leaves hung on the trees ready to flutter down at the slightest puff of air; the great bushes of Michaelmas daisies in the kitchen-garden were making their last show of flowers. We must needs taste the fruit off the different trees, and pass our judgment as to their flavour; and we went away with our pockets stuffed with those that we liked best. As we had passed to the orchard, Holdsworth had admired and spoken about some flower which he saw; it so happened he had never seen this old-fashioned kind since the days of his boyhood. I do not know whether he had thought anything more about this chance speech of his, but I know I had not – when Phillis, who had been missing just at the last moment of our hurried visit, re-appeared with a little nosegay of this same flower, which she was tying up with a blade of grass. She offered it to Holdsworth as he stood with her father on the point of departure. I saw their faces. I saw for the first time an unmistakable look of love in his black eyes; it was more than gratitude for the little attention; it was tender and beseeching – passionate.

Cousin Phillis, ELIZABETH GASKELL 1812 65

THE PROGRESS OF LOVE

Beneath the myrtle's secret shade,
  When Delia blessed my eyes;
At first I viewed the lovely maid
  In silent soft surprise.
With trembling voice, and anxious mind,
  I softly whispered love;
She blushed a smile so sweetly kind,
  Did all my fears remove.
Her lovely yielding form I pressed,
  Sweet maddening kisses stole;
And soon her swimming eyes confessed
  The wishes of her soul:
In wild tumultuous bliss, I cry,
  'O Delia, now be kind!'
She pressed me close, and with a sigh,
  To melting joys resigned.

ROBERT DODSLEY 1703–64

[34]

*M*Y LOVELY GARDEN

The tulip, jas'min, emony, and rose,
Of which we'll garlands for thy head compose.
Nature to make my fountain, did its part,
Which ever flows without the help of Art,
A faithful mirror shall its water be,
Where thou may'st sit beneath a shady tree.

PHILIP AYRES 1638–1712

[35]

$\mathcal{S}$ILENT NOON

•◆•

Your hands lie open in the long fresh grass, –
  The finger-points look through like rosy blooms;
  Your eyes smile peace. The pasture gleams and glooms
'Neath billowing skies that scatter and amass.
All round our nest, far as the eye can pass,
  Are golden kingcup-fields with silver edge
  Where the cow-parsley skirts the hawthorn-hedge.
'Tis visible silence, still as the hour-glass.

DANTE GABRIEL ROSSETTI 1828–82

$\mathcal{L}$OVERS' LANE

Come, come, my love, the bush is growing.
    The linnet sings the tune again
He sung when thou with garments flowing
    Went talking with me down the lane.
Dreaming of beauty ere I found thee,
    And musing by the bushes green;
The wind, enamoured, streaming round thee
    Painted the visions I had seen.

I guessed thy face without the knowing
    Was beautiful as e'er was seen;
I thought so by thy garments flowing
    And gait as airy as a queen;
Thy shape, thy size, could not deceive me:
    Beauty seemed hid in every limb;
And then thy face, when seen, believe me,
    Made every former fancy dim.

Yes, when thy face in beauty brightened
    The music of a voice divine,
Upon my heart thy sweetness lightened;
    Life, love, that moment, all were thine;
All I imagined musing lonely,
    When dreaming 'neath the greenwood tree,
Seeming to fancy visions only,
    Breathed living when I met with thee.

And on that long-remembered morning
  When first I lost this heart of mine,
Fame, all I'd hoped for, turned to scorning
  And love and hope lived wholly thine;
I told thee, and with rapture glowing
  I heard thee more than once declare,
That down the lane with garments flowing
  Thou with the spring wouldst wander there.

JOHN CLARE 1793–1864

[39]

 Y RESTING PLACE

Farewell to one now silenced quite,
Sent out of hearing, out of sight, –
    My friend of friends, whom I shall miss.
    He is not banished, though, for this, –
Nor he, nor sadness, nor delight.

Though I shall walk with him no more,
A low voice sounds upon the shore.
    He must not watch my resting-place
    But who shall drive a mournful face
From the sad winds about my door?

I shall not hear his voice complain
But who shall stop the patient rain?
    His tears must not disturb my heart,
    But who shall change the years, and part
The world from every thought of pain?

He is not banished, for the showers
Yet wake this green warm earth of ours.
    How can the summer but be sweet?
    I shall not have him at my feet,
And yet my feet are on the flowers.

ALICE MEYNELL 1847–1922

$\mathcal{T}$HE BLOOM OF THE YEAR

All the breath and the bloom of the
    year in the bag of one bee:
All the wonder and wealth of the mine in
    the heart of one gem:
In the core of one pearl all the shade and the
    shine of the sea:
Breath and bloom, shade and shine, – wonder,
    wealth, and – how far above them –
        Truth, that's brighter than gem,
        Trust, that's purer than pearl, –
Brightest truth, purest trust in the universe –
        all were for me
            In the kiss of one girl.

ROBERT BROWNING 1812–89

THE BLESSÈD DAMOZEL

The blessèd damozel lean'd out
   From the gold bar of Heaven;
Her eyes were deeper than the depth
   Of waters still'd at even;
She had three lilies in her hand,
   And the stars in her hair were seven.

Her robe, ungirt from clasp to hem,
   No wrought flowers did adorn,
But a white rose of Mary's gift,
   For service meetly worn;
Her hair that lay along her back
   Was yellow like ripe corn.

DANTE GABRIEL ROSSETTI 1828–82

The Rose Bower

Sweet, serene, sky-like flower,
Haste to adorn her bower,
From thy long cloudy bed
Shoot forth thy damask head.

Vermilion ball that's given
From lip to lip in heaven,
Love's couch's coverled,
Haste, haste to make her bed.

RICHARD LOVELACE 1618–58

THE TRYST

Clym took the hand which was already bared for him – it was a favourite way with them to walk bare hand in bare hand – and led her through the ferns. They formed a very comely picture of love at full flush, as they walked along the valley that late afternoon, the sun sloping down on their right, and throwing their thin spectral shadows, tall as poplar trees, far out across the furze and fern. Eustacia went with her head thrown back fancifully, a certain glad and voluptuous air of triumph pervading her eyes at having won by her own unaided self a man who was her perfect complement in attainments, appearance, and age. On the young man's part, the paleness of face which he had brought with him from Paris, and the incipient marks of time and thought, were less perceptible than when he returned, the healthful and energetic sturdiness which was his by nature having partially recovered its original proportions. They wandered onward till they reached the nether margin of the heath, where it became marshy, and merged in moorland.

'I must part from you here, Clym,' said Eustacia.

They stood still and prepared to bid each other farewell. Everything before them was on a perfect level. The sun, resting on the horizon line, streamed across the ground from between copper-coloured and lilac clouds, stretched out in flats beneath a sky of pale soft green. All dark objects on the earth that lay towards the sun were overspread by a purple haze, against which groups of wailing gnats shone out, rising upwards and dancing about like sparks of fire.

'O! this leaving you is too hard to bear!' exclaimed Eustacia in a sudden whisper of anguish. 'Your mother will influence you too much; I shall not be judged fairly, it will get afloat that I am not a good girl, and the witch story will be added to make me blacker!'

'They cannot. Nobody dares to speak disrespectfully of you or of me.'

'O how I wish I was sure of never losing you – that you could not be able to desert me anyhow!'

Clym stood silent a moment. His feelings were high, the moment was passionate, and he cut the knot.

'You shall be sure of me, darling,' he said, folding her in his arms. 'We will be married at once.'

'O Clym!'

The Return of the Native, THOMAS HARDY 1840–1928

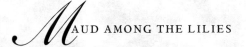Maud among the Lilies

Birds in the high Hall-garden
    When twilight was falling,
Maud, Maud, Maud, Maud,
    They were crying and calling.

Where was Maud? in our wood;
    And I, who else, was with her,
Gathering woodland lilies,
    Myriads blow together.

Birds in our wood sang
    Ringing thro' the vallies,
Maud is here, here, here
    In among the lilies.

I kiss'd her slender hand,
    She took the kiss sedately;
Maud is not seventeen,
    But she is tall and stately.

I to cry out on pride
    Who have won her favour!
O Maud were sure of Heaven
    If lowliness could save her.

I know the way she went
    Home with her maiden posy,
For her feet have touch'd the meadows
    And left the daisies rosy.

Birds in the high Hall-garden
    Were crying and calling to her,
Where is Maud, Maud, Maud,
    One is come to woo her.

ALFRED, LORD TENNYSON 1809–92

PHILLADA FLOUTS ME

O what a plague is love!
  How shall I bear it?
She will inconstant prove,
  I greatly fear it.
She so torments my mind
  That my strength faileth,
And wavers with the wind
  As a ship saileth.
Please her the best I may,
She loves still to gainsay;
Alack and well-a-day!
  Phillada flouts me.

In the last month of May
  I made her posies;
I heard her often say
  That she loved roses.
Cowslips and gillyflowers
  And the white lily
I brought to deck the bowers
  For my sweet Philly.
But she did all disdain,
And threw them back again;
Therefore 'tis flat and plain
  Phillada flouts me.

ANONYMOUS SEVENTEENTH CENTURY

To A YOUNG LADY

 Sweet stream, that winds through yonder glade,
Apt emblem of a virtuous maid –
Silent and chaste she steals along,
Far from the world's gay busy throng:
With gentle yet prevailing force,
Intent upon her destined course;
Graceful and useful all she does,
Blessing and blest where'er she goes;
Pure-bosom'd as that watery glass,
And Heaven reflected in her face.

WILLIAM COWPER 1731–1800

# To THESE GARDENS GAVE

'Tis she that to these gardens gave
That wondrous beauty which they have;
She straightness on the woods bestows;
To her the meadow sweetness owes;
Nothing could make the river be
So crystal pure but only she;
She yet more pure, sweet, straight, and fair,
Than gardens, woods, meads, rivers are.

Therefore what first she on them spent,
They gratefully again present:
The meadow, carpets where to tread;
The garden, flowers to crown her head;
And for a glass, the limpid brook,
Where she may all her beauties look;
But, since she would not have them seen,
The wood about her draws a screen.

ANDREW MARVELL 1621–78

A DREAM

I dreamed that, as I wandered by the way,
  Bare Winter suddenly was changed to Spring,
And gentle odours led my steps astray,
  Mixed with a sound of waters murmuring
Along a shelving bank of turf, which lay
  Under a copse, and hardly dared to fling
Its green arms round the bosom of the stream,
But kissed it and then fled, as thou mightest in a dream.

PERCY BYSSHE SHELLEY 1792–1822

THE LOVER

Henceforth I will not set my love
    On other than the country lass,
For in the court I see and prove
    Fancy is brittle as the glass.
The love bestowed on the great
    Is ever full of toil and cares,

Subject still to frown and freat,
   With sugar'd baits in subtle snares.
In good old times it was the guise
   To show things in their proper kind,
Love painted out in naked wise
   To show his plain and single mind.
But since into the court he came
   Infected with a braver style
He lost both property and name,
   Attired all in craft and guile.
Yet in the village still he keeps,
   And merry makes with little cost,
But never breaks their quiet sleeps
   With jealous thoughts or labour lost.
What though in silver and in gold
   The bonny lass be not so brave
Yet are her looks fresh to behold
   And that is it that love doth crave.
Fair fall the petticoat of red
   That veils the skin as white as milk,
And such as would not so be sped
   Let them go coy the gowns of silk.
Keep, ladies, keep for your own turns
   The Spanish red to mend your looks,
For when the sun my Daphne burns
   She seeks the water of the brooks,
And though the musk and amber fine
   So ladylike she cannot get,
Yet will she wear the sweet woodbine,
   The primrose and the violet.

SIR ARTHUR GORGES 1577–1625

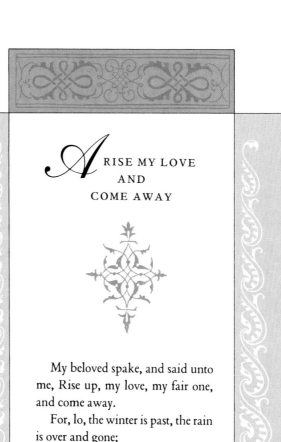

ARISE MY LOVE AND COME AWAY

My beloved spake, and said unto me, Rise up, my love, my fair one, and come away.

For, lo, the winter is past, the rain is over and gone;

The flowers appear on the earth; the time of the singing of birds is come, and the voice of the turtle is heard in our land:

The fig tree putteth forth her green figs, and the vines with the tender grape give a good smell. Arise, my love, my fair one, and come away.

OLD TESTAMENT

$\mathcal{T}$O WANDER UNSEEN

It was now the sweetest hour of the twenty-four: 'day its fervid fires had wasted', and dew fell cool on panting plain and scorched summit. Where the sun had gone down in simple state – pure of the pomp of clouds – spread a solemn purple, burning with the light of red jewel and furnace flame at one point, on one hill-peak, and extending high and wide, soft and still softer, over half heaven. The east had its own charm of fine, deep blue, and its own modest gem, a rising and solitary star: soon it would boast the moon; but she was yet beneath the horizon.

I walked a while on the pavement; but a subtle, well-known scent — that of a cigar — stole from some window; I saw the library casement open a hand-breadth; I knew I might be watched thence; so I went apart into the orchard. No nook in the grounds more sheltered and more Eden-like; a very high wall shut it out from the court on one side; on the other a beech avenue screened it from the lawn. At the bottom was a sunk fence, its sole separation from lonely fields: a winding walk, bordered with laurels and terminating in a giant horse-chestnut, circled at the base by a seat, led down to the fence. Here one could wander unseen. While such honeydew fell, such silence reigned, such gloaming gathered, I felt as if I could haunt such shade for ever; but in treading the flower and fruit parterres at the upper part of the enclosure, enticed there by the light the now rising moon cast on this more open quarter, my step is stayed — not by sound, not by sight, but once more by a warning fragrance.

Sweet-brier and southernwood, jasmine, pink, and rose have long been yielding their evening sacrifice of incense: this new scent is neither of shrub nor flower; it is — I know it well — it is Mr Rochester's cigar. I look round and listen. I see trees laden with ripening fruit. I hear a nightingale warbling in a wood half a mile off: no moving form is visible, no coming step audible; but that perfume increases: I must flee. I make for the wicket leading to the shrubbery, and I see Mr Rochester entering. I step aside into the ivy recess; he will not stay long: he will soon return whence he came, and if I sit still he will never see me.

Jane Eyre, CHARLOTTE BRONTË 1816-55

[63]

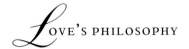 ##OVE'S PHILOSOPHY

The fountains mingle with the river,
　　And the rivers with the ocean;
The winds of heaven mix forever,
　　With a sweet emotion;
Nothing in the world is single;
　　All things by a law divine
In one another's being mingle:–
　　Why not I with thine?

See! the mountains kiss high heaven
　　And the waves clasp one another;
No sister flower would be forgiven
　　If it disdained its brother;
And the sunlight clasps the earth,
　　And the moonbeams kiss the sea:–
What are all these kissings worth,
　　If thou kiss not me?

PERCY BYSSHE SHELLEY 1792–1822

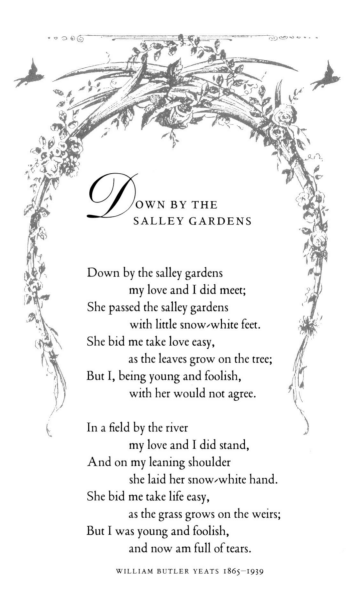

DOWN BY THE SALLEY GARDENS

Down by the salley gardens
    my love and I did meet;
She passed the salley gardens
    with little snow‑white feet.
She bid me take love easy,
    as the leaves grow on the tree;
But I, being young and foolish,
    with her would not agree.

In a field by the river
    my love and I did stand,
And on my leaning shoulder
    she laid her snow‑white hand.
She bid me take life easy,
    as the grass grows on the weirs;
But I was young and foolish,
    and now am full of tears.

WILLIAM BUTLER YEATS 1865–1939

BEAUTIFUL LADIES

Beautiful ladies through the orchard pass;
Bend under crutched-up branches, forked and low;
Trailing their samet palls o'er dew-drenched grass.

Pale blossoms, looking on proud Jacqueline,
Blush to the colour of her finger tips,
And rosy knuckles, laced with yellow lace.

High-crested Berthe discerns, with slant, clinched eyes,
Amid the leaves pink faces of the skies;
She locks her plaintive hands Sainte-Margot-wise.

Ysabeau follows last, with languorous pace;
Presses, voluptuous, to her bursting lips,
With backward stoop, a branch of eglantine.

Courtly ladies through the orchard pass;
Bow low, as in lords' halls; and springtime grass
Tangles a snare to catch the tapering toe.

JOHN GRAY 1866-1934

REFLECTIONS

She turned her face to where the load of virginal blossom, whiter than summer-cloud on the sky, showered and drooped and clustered so thick as to claim colour and seem, like higher Alpine snows in noon-sunlight, a flush of white. From deep to deeper heavens of white, her eyes perched and soared. Wonder lived in her. Happiness in the beauty of the tree pressed to supplant it, and was more mortal and narrower. Reflection came, contracting her vision and weighing her to earth. Her reflection was: 'He must be good who loves to lie and sleep beneath the branches of this tree!'

GEORGE MEREDITH 1828–1909

*H*IGH MIDSUMMER

Soon will the high Midsummer pomps come on,
　　Soon will the musk carnations break and swell,
Soon shall we have gold-dusted snapdragon,
　　Sweet-William with his homely cottage-smell,
　　And stocks in fragrant blow;
Roses that down the alleys shine afar,
　　And open, jasmine-muddled lattices,
　　And groups under the dreaming garden-trees,
And the full moon, and the white evening-star.

MATTHEW ARNOLD 1822–88

THE BEST FLOWERS

The timid maid,
Pleased to be praised, and yet of praise afraid,
Seeks the best flowers; not those of wood and fields,
But such as every farmer's garden yields —
Fine cabbage-roses, painted like her face,
The shining pansy, trimm'd with golden lace,
The tall-topped larkheels, feather'd thick with flowers,
The woodbine, climbing o'er the door in bowers,
The London tufts, of many a mottled hue,
The pale pink pea, and monkshood darkly blue,
The white and purple gilliflowers, that stay
Ling'ring, in blossom, summer half away,
The single blood-walls, of a luscious smell,
Old-fashion'd flowers which housewives love so well,
The columbines, stone-blue, or deep night-brown,
Their honeycomb-like blossoms hanging down
Each cottage-garden's fond adopted child,
Though heaths still claim them, where they yet grow wild.

JOHN CLARE 1793–1864

# THE SPOUSAL TIME OF MAY

'Twas when the spousal time of May
    Hangs all the hedge with bridal wreaths,
And air's so sweet the bosom gay
    Gives thanks for every breath it breathes;
When like to like is gladly moved,
    And each thing joins in Spring's refrain,
'Let those love now who never loved;
    'Let those who have loved love again;'
That I, in whom the sweet time wrought,
    Lay stretch'd within a lonely glade,
Abandon'd to delicious thought,
    Beneath the softly twinkling shade.
The leaves, all stirring, mimick'd well
    A neighbouring rush of rivers cold,
And, as the sun or shadow fell,
    So these were green and those were gold;
In dim recesses hyacinths droop'd,
    And breadths of primrose lit the air,
Which, wandering through the woodland, stoop'd
    And gather'd perfumes here and there;
Upon the spray the squirrel swung,
    And careless songsters, six or seven,
Sang lofty songs the leaves among,
    Fit for their only listener, Heaven.

COVENTRY PATMORE 1823–96

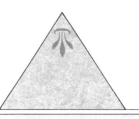

$\mathcal{M}$Y GREENHOUSE

My dear,
I will not let you come till the
end of May or beginning of
June, because before that time
my greenhouse will not be
ready to receive us, and it is the
only pleasant room belonging
to us. When the plants go out
we go in. I line it with mats,
and spread the floor with mats;
and there you shall sit with a
bed of mignonette at your side,
and a hedge of honeysuckles,
roses, and jasmine; and I will
make you a bouquet of myrtle
every day.

WILLIAM COWPER 1731–1800

PHILLIS WALKS AMID HER
GARDEN ALLEYS

Sweet birds, that sit and sing amid the shady valleys,
And see how sweetly Phillis walks amid her garden alleys,
Go round about her bower, and sing as ye are bidden:
To her is only known his faith that from the world is hidden.
And she among you all that hath the sweetest voice,
Go chirp of him that never told, yet never changed, his choice.

And not forget his faith that lived for ever loved,
Yet never made his fancy known, nor ever favour moved;
And ever let your ground of all your grace be this —
'To you, to you, to you the due of love and honour is,
On you, on you, on you our music all attendeth,
For as on you our Muse begun, in you all music endeth.'

NICHOLAS BRETON 1545?—1626?

Under the Tree

'This was a favourite tree with my dear father,' said she: 'he used to love to sit under its foliage, with his family about him, in the fine evenings of summer.'

Valancourt understood her feelings, and was silent: had she raised her eyes from the ground, she would have seen tears in his. He rose, and leaned on the wall of the terrace; from which in a few moments he returned to his seat; then rose again, and appeared to be greatly agitated; while Emily found her spirits so much depressed, that several of her attempts to renew the conversation were ineffectual. Valancourt again sat down; but was still silent, and trembled. At length he said with a hesitating voice, 'This lovely scene I am going to leave! – to leave you – perhaps for ever! These moments may never return! I cannot resolve to neglect, though I scarcely dare to avail myself of them. Let me, however, without offending the delicacy of your sorrow, venture to declare the admiration I must always feel of your goodness – oh! that at some future period I might be permitted to call it love!'

ANN RADCLIFFE 1764–1823

SHE WALKS AMONG LOVELINESS

She walks among the loveliness she made,
Between the apple-blossom and the water —
She walks among the patterned pied brocade,
Each flower her son and every tree her daughter.

V. SACKVILLE-WEST 1892–1962

TO AMANDA WALKING IN THE GARDEN

And now what monarch would not gardener be,
My fair Amanda's stately gait to see?
How her feet tempt! how soft and light she treads,
Fearing to wake the flowers from their beds!
Yet from their sweet green pillows everywhere
They start and gaze about to see my Fair.
Look at yon flower yonder, how it grows,
Sensibly! how it opes its leaves and blows,
Puts its best Easter clothes on, neat and gay:
No herb, pressed by her foot, but blossoms straight;
Flowers, for her touch to ripen them, do wait;
They, from her hand, new fragrancy do yield;
Her presence fills with perfumes all the field.

NICHOLAS HOOKES 1628–1712

$\mathcal{S}$UMMER PURSUITS

So now you walked beside an odorous bed
Of gorgeous hues, white, azure, golden, red;
And now turned off into a leafy walk,
Close and continuous, fit for lovers' talk;
And now pursued the stream, and as you trod
Onward and onward o'er the velvet sod,
Felt on your face an air, watery and sweet,
And a new sense in your self-lighting feet;
And then perhaps you entered upon shades,
Pillowed with dells and uplands 'twixt the glades,
Through which the distant palace, now and then,
Looked lordly forth with many-windowed ken;
A land of trees, which reaching round about,
In shady blessing stretched their old arms out,
With spots of sunny opening, and with nooks,
To lie and read in, sloping into brooks,
Where at her drink you started the slim deer.

JAMES HENRY LEIGH HUNT 1784–1859

I KNOW A
LITTLE GARDEN

I know a little garden close
Set thick with lily and red rose,
Where I would wander if I might
From dewy dawn to dewy night,
And have one with me wandering.

WILLIAM MORRIS 1834–96

 IME OF ROSES

It was not in the Winter
    Our loving lot was cast;
It was the time of roses –
    We pluck'd them as we pass'd!

That churlish season never frown'd
    On early lovers yet:
O no – the world was newly crown'd
    With flowers when first we met!

'Twas twilight, and I bade you go,
    But still you held me fast;
It was the time of roses –
    We pluck'd them as we pass'd!

THOMAS HOOD 1835–74

LILAC FAIR

O were my Love yon lilac fair,
  Wi' purple blossoms to the spring,
And I a bird to shelter there,
  When wearied on my little wing;
How I wad mourn when it was torn
  By autumn wild and winter rude!
But I wad sing on wanton wing
  When youthfu' May its bloom renew'd.

ROBERT BURNS 1759–96

LIST OF PAINTINGS

Slipcase and Frontispiece (detail): *The Rector's Garden: Queen of the Lilies*, J. A. Grimshaw; Cover: *Bouquet de Fleurs*, Pierre-Joseph Redouté; p. 4 19thC. Valentine Card; pp. 6–7 *Engaged*, T. R. W. S. Lloyd; p. 8 *Spring*, A. Stevens; p. 11 *Ophelia*, J. W. Waterhouse; p. 12 *Mr and Mrs Auchmutz and their son* (detail), C. W. Cope; p. 13 *July flowers, Oaklands Rugeley* (detail), B. Parsons; p. 15 *Bright Summer*, M. Stone; pp. 16–17 *A. Woodland Idyll* (detail), A. Hlavacek; p. 18 *The Garden*, E. Walker; p. 20 *Early Summer* (detail), A. Woolmer; p. 21 *Bol de Roses*, H. Fantin-Latour; p. 23 *Quiet*, E. Killingworth Johnson; p. 24 *The Princess and the Frog*, E. J. Poynter; p. 26 *A Stolen Rose*, F. Cipolla; p. 27 *The Squire's Daughter* (detail), A. Glendening; p. 28 *The Parasol*, A. Hacker; p. 30 *Little Finger Tell Me True*, E. Killingworth Johnson; p. 32 *The Orchard*, N. Erichsen; p. 34 *A Romantic Meeting* (detail), F. Andreotti; p. 35 *Summer Time* (detail), L. Stannard; p. 36 *A Summer's Day*, E. Killingworth Johnson; p. 39 *Lover's Lane*, F. Vigers; p. 40 *Faraway Thoughts* (detail) Anon; p. 42 *Yew Arches, Murthy Castle, Perthshire* (detail), G. S. Elgood; p. 43 *Cloister Lilies*, M. Spartali Stillman; p. 44 *The Rose Bower*, H. Zatzka; p. 46 *The Tryst*, A. Hughes; p. 49 'Our Ladies Flower's *Madonna Lilies and Roses* (detail), B. Parsons; p. 50 '*Off*', E. Blair Leighton; p. 52 *L'Été*, A. Lynch; p. 55 *A Garden in Tangiers*, J. Lavery; p. 56–7 *Picking Wild Flowers*, A. Glendening; p. 58 *The Lover's Return*, M. Stone; p. 61 *Blossoms*, A. Drummond; p. 62 *The Old Gateway*, T. Mostyn; p. 64 *From The Miller's Daughter by Tennyson*, J. A. Vintner; p. 67 *Picking Roses*, J. A. Marioton; p. 68 *Women in a Garden*, C. Monet; p. 70 *In The Spring*, H. Knight; p. 71 *Summer Border* (detail), B. Parsons; p. 72 *Pot-Pourri*, E. Killingworth Johnson; p. 74 *The Garden Figure*, A. Stanhope Forbes; p. 77 *A Young Lady in a Conservatory*, J. M. Bowkett; p. 78 *The Last Summer Days*, T. Brooks; p. 81 *A Picnic In The Park*, T. Creswick; p. 82 *Springtime*, D. Woodlock; p. 84–5 *Lady In The Garden*, C. Monet; p. 86 *A Summer Afternoon*, J. R. Skelton; p. 88 *The Rose Walk*, E. H. Adie; p. 89 *Picking Roses*, R. J.Gordon; p. 91 *Spring: Mrs Newton in the Garden*, J. J. J. Tissot.

Anonymous *Phillada Flouts Me*, p. 50; Valentine p. 27. Matthew
Arnold, from *Thyrsis* p. 71. Philip Ayres, *Invites his Nymph to his
Cottage* p. 35. Elizabeth Barrett Browning, *Spring* p. 17. Nicholas
Breton, *Sweet birds, that sit and sing amid the Shady Valleys* p. 79.
Charlotte Brontë, from *Jane Eyre* p. 62. Robert Burns, *O were my
Love yon Lilac Fair* p. 90. John Clare, *First Love* p. 20; *With
Garments Flowing* p. 38; from *Poems Descriptive of Rural Life: A
Cottage Poem* p. 73. William Cowper, *To a Young Lady* p. 52;
Letter to Lady Hesketh dated 9.2.1786 p. 76. Robert Dodsley, *The
Progress of Love* p. 34. Giles Fletcher, *If any ask why roses please the
sight* p. 7. Elizabeth Gaskell, from *Cousin Phillis* p. 33. Sir Arthur
Gorges, from *The Lover's Return* p. 58. Thomas Hardy, from *The
Return of the Native* p. 46. Robert Herrick, *The Tear sent to her from
Staines* p. 29. Thomas Hood, *Time of Roses* p. 89. Nicholas
Hookes, *To Amanda Walking in the Garden* p. 85. James Henry
Leigh Hunt, from *The Story of Rimini* p. 87. Rev. Francis Kilvert,
Entry from his Diary dated 18.9.1871 p. 14. Richard Leigh,
Gathering Peaches p. 18. Thomas Lodge, *Turn I my Looks* p. 22.
Richard Lovelace, *The Rose* p. 44. Andrew Marvell, *The Garden*
p. 30; from *Upon Appleton House* p. 54. George Meredith, from *The
Egoist* p. 70. Alice Meynell *Parted* p. 41. William Morris, from *The
Life and Death of Jason* p. 88. John Bowyer Buchanan Nichols,
Amoret p. 9. Old Testament from *The Song of Solomon* p. 60. John
Boyle O'Reilly *A White Rose* p. 26. Coventry Patmore, *'Twas when
the spousal time of May* p. 75. Edgar Alan Poe, *Summum Bonum* p. 42.
Ann Radcliffe, from *The Mysteries of Udolpho* p. 80. Dante Gabriel
Rosseti, *Silent Noon* p. 37; *The Blessèd Damozel* p. 43. Percy Byssche
Shelley from *The Question* p. 57; *Love's Philosophy* p. 65. V.
Sackville-West, *Rabbits* dated 1.2.44 p. 12; from *The Land* p. 83.
William Shakespeare, *Ophelia's Song* p. 10. Lord Alfred Tennyson,
from *Maud* p. 48. William Wordsworth, *Louisa* p. 24. William
Butler Yeats, *Down by the Salley Gardens* p. 66.

PICTURE ACKNOWLEDGEMENTS

The publishers wish to thank the following for permission to reproduce the illustrations: Ashmolean Museum, Oxford p. 43. Bridgeman Art Library, London, with acknowledgements to: Chris Beetles, London pp. 6–7; Guildhall Art Gallery, London p. 8; Christopher Wood Gallery, London pp. 12, 35, 71, 86; Private Collections pp. 13, 16–17; Bradford Art Galleries and Museums p. 18; Waterhouse and Dodd, London p. 20; Roy Miles Fine Paintings, London pp. 32, 77; Josef Mensing Gallery, Hamm-Rhynern p. 44; Wolverhampton Art Gallery p. 64; Musée D'Orsay, Paris p. 68; Hermitage, Leningrad pp. 84–5; Christies, London pp. 11, 91; Lindley Library, Royal Horticultural Society, London, Cover. Christie's Colour Library, London with acknowledgements to: Eugene Edelman, Los Angeles p. 61; Private Collection p. 67. Mary Evans Picture Library, London p. 4. Fine Art Photographic Library, London pp. 15, 21, 23, 24, 26, 28, 30, 36, 39, 40, 52, 56–7, 58, 72, 78, 81, 82. Harris Museum and Art Gallery, Preston, Lancashire, Slipcase and Frontispiece (detail). Laing Art Gallery, Newcastle upon Tyne (Tyne and Wear Museums Service) p. 70. Maas Gallery, London p. 27. Manchester City Art Galleries p. 50. Photographs courtesy of David Messum Fine Paintings, London WI pp. 55, 62, 74. Newlyn Orion p. 74. Tate Gallery, London p. 46, Photographs by courtesy of Christopher Wood Gallery, London pp. 42, 49, 88, 89.

DEAR FRIEND, FOR YOUR PLEASURE
THE PAGES OF THIS TREASURY
OF ROMANTIC VERSE HAVE BEEN
SPECIALLY SCENTED WITH THE
BEAUTIFUL FRAGRANCE
OF VICTORIA, THE SIGNATURE
PERFUME OF VICTORIA'S SECRET.

*V*ICTORIA